A Short Glossary of Drinking Game Terms

Communal cup = A centrally located cup into which all players add beverage and from which the unlucky ones take it away.

Personal cup = A cup that, although located on the central playing field, is yours only to drink from.

Shooter = The player whose turn it is. This term is found mostly in dice and quarters games.

Social Drink = Everyone enjoys a mid-sized sip.

Beer bong = A funnel with a long tube connected to the bottom, into which one pours beer. The participator then puts the tube to his lips, his friend lifts the funnel, he drinks it fast, madness ensues.

PUBLISHER'S DISCLAIMER FOR
50 Great College Drinking Games

The games described in this book are intended only for adults. Drinking and driving are dangerous, and these games should not be played by anyone who is planning on driving. Excessive and rapid consumption of alcoholic beverages can cause injury and even death, and persistent use can lead to alcoholism. Readers are therefore cautioned to use good judgment in playing these games. Neither the author nor the publisher assumes any liability for any injury that may arise as a result of playing these games.

ATTENTION: ORGANIZATIONS AND CORPORATIONS

Most HarperPaperbacks are available at special quantity discounts for bulk purchases for sales promotions, premiums, or fund-raising. For information, please call or write:
Special Markets Department, HarperCollins*Publishers*,
10 East 53rd Street, New York, N.Y. 10022.
Telephone: (212) 207-7528. Fax: (212) 207-7222.

50 Great College Drinking Games

ROSS BONANDER

HarperPaperbacks
A Division of HarperCollinsPublishers

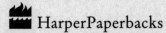

HarperPaperbacks

A Division of HarperCollins*Publishers*
10 East 53rd Street, New York, N.Y. 10022-5299

If you purchased this book without a cover, you should be aware
that this book is stolen property. It was reported as "unsold and
destroyed" to the publisher and neither the author nor the
publisher has received any payment for this "stripped book."

Copyright © 1997 by Ross Bonander
All rights reserved. No part of this book may be used or
reproduced in any manner whatsoever without written
permission of the publisher, except in the case of brief
quotations embodied in critical articles and reviews.
For information address HarperCollins*Publishers,*
10 East 53rd Street, New York, N.Y. 10022-5299.

ISBN 0-06-101171-1

HarperCollins®, ✠®, and HarperPaperbacks™
are trademarks of HarperCollins*Publishers,* Inc.

Cover design by Rich Rossiter

First printing: September 1997

Printed in the United States of America

Visit HarperPaperbacks on the World Wide Web at
http://www.harpercollins.com

❖ 10 9 8 7 6 5 4 3 2 1

Acknowledgments

The Band would like to thank (in no particular order): Matt Becher, "Damaged" Dan Fedorenko, Allison Marshall, Sharon Hendrickson, Carl "Torture" Cole, Meredith Deas, Lic "Vic" Belonogoff (for all those killer riffs), Jason Pronos, Dave Fedorenko and all the guys in False Utopia, Jennifer Messick, The Hammer Bonander and Melissa, Mike Messick, Heather Genschmer, Todd Calvert, Andrew Roy for his faith in Vice Grip, Mary Saporito, and Ken "Liver Damage" Marden of Waterville. And to all our friends and fans around the world . . . up the Irons and rock on! We'll see you on the Hell to Pay tour coming soon to a venue near you!

To Jeff Rutherford

Finally, to Mom and Dad

Table of Contents

The Classic Game of Quarters and Its Aggressive Offspring

> Quarters
> Speed Quarters
> Chandeliers
> Spin Quarters
> Anchor-Man
> Game Day
> QP^2

Games Involving the Enigmatic Deck of Cards

> Up the River, Down the River
> Blind Man's Bullshit
> Asshole
> Horse Races
> King's Cup
> Cops and Pushers
> Suck and Blow
> Spoons
> Suck the Sock

CHAPTER 6
Hard-core & Hellish 83
Games Geared Toward Kicking Your Ass

CHAPTER 7
Miscellaneous Mayhem 94
Games Whose Rules Fit No Particular Chapter

Introduction

"It has no meaning to say that a game has always been played wrong."
—Wittgenstein, *On Certainty*

It almost seems as though, through the ages, rules for drinking games have been so loose that anything counted, so long as a cup was in your hand, somebody yelled "drink!" and you did. But c'mon folks, this is too unrestricted! If it was all we needed, I'd have to include games like Point, where you point at your opponent and she drinks; Pound, where you do just that; and Recliner, where you call yourself a lazy piece of shit and cash a cheap twelve-pack in front of reruns after work every evening. While all three suggested games are pretty sorry, the particular tragedy of Recliner is that it would be a game with no winners, only losers . . . which is really close to the overall description of every drinking game. Hmm.

Drinking games, as silly as it may sound, pervade the popular culture; in fact, they reflect it. When fraternity parties were out of control and often freely sanctioned by the university during the *Animal House/Revenge of the Nerds* era, ferocious games like Beer Die and Anchor-Man ruled with an iron fist. While that anarchic mentality has been replaced by an academically driven moderationism, and while you may find that some of our older, more distinguished drinking game peers use outdated references ("Drink it down, you brace-faced moron!"), the collective spirit is still the same. This is evident in games like Quarters, which is such an icon of the establishment that it has remained secure in its path over shifting trends and the chameleon mass conscience better than Dick Clark or a shelved Twinkie.

But while that's just dandy, don't get *too* good at any one game. Don't excel or strive or, God forbid, call yourself a "pro" with any sense of pride. That's depressing. All things in moderation, right? Let the tragedy of every drooping beer belly speak this wisdom to you as an example. Imagine where we could be if Recliner hadn't sapped us of our spirits, compared to where many of us are now: crushing empty cans of Blatz beer against the forehead amidst the zany double entendres of *Three's Company* reruns, wishing we were sippin' our suds at the Regal Beagle with Mr. Roper. If our culture is connecting with Stanley, we've got problems that are plainly too big for this book.

Also, remember that all drinking game rules are malleable, stated here only to give you a starting point. If you can think of a better adaptation, let it ride, my friend. Let it ride. Contort the rules and make up a whole new game; make it better if you can. Drinking games, in accordance with Wittgenstein, are not set in stone. This transcendent, authority-free nature is a prime reason why they still rock. They're ready to wind through the ages armed with elastic borders so that you can do what you want with them.

Years later, the simple adaptations you make will mesh with other changes and will, Darwinlike, build us a better drunk tank; a more efficient machine to run us down the assembly line and stamp us, at the very least, "amused."

Finally, drinking games go well with rock 'n' roll, because both are indulgent and decadent, both get your blood pressure up, and neither win your parents' approval. I myself started out stuck in three power chords, playing a sorry Gibson Epiphone along to the boring, cliché-ridden soft rock scene, all while sipping my generic label beer without an ounce of passion for life. Then I came upon drinking games and, as though they were intertwined, discovered rock 'n' roll. Look at me now: an American success story armed with a gorgeous ebony Les Paul and hours of Beer Die to my credit. Now, since I've written the book, all that's left for me is rock 'n' roll stardom. If you wanna be like me, don't forget to fire up the stereo before sitting down at the table, making sure that whatever you choose is heavy on the distortion and steeped deep in the rhythm of danger.

Having said that, I present fifty drinking games to challenge and entertain. Every game has been feverishly tested, retested, then approved for the drinking age public by a discerning staff led by me, your virile and gracious guide on this sometimes uneasy expedition. I give you games representing California and the Pacific Northwest; Las Vegas, Nevada; Texas; Mississippi; Georgetown, District of Columbia; and New England;

to name a few, and even a tiny sample from our Canadian neighbors to the north and our friendly mates Down Under. So turn the page, raise your fist, hold up a flickering lighter if you must, and get ready to bang yer head to the blistering heavy metal shards and rock 'n' roll remains of some truly great college drinking games.

Terms to Grasp

A short list of terms is provided to help you on your journey.

Communal cup: A centrally located cup into which all players add beverage and from which the unlucky ones take it away.

Personal cup: A cup that, although located on the central playing field, is yours only to drink from.

Shooter: In dice and quarter games, the player whose turn it is.

Social Drink: Everyone enjoys a mid-sized sip.

X: The variable. You can determine the variable by determining how many players will be participating in your chosen game.

Beer Bong: A funnel with a long tube connected to the bottom, into which one pours beer. The participator then puts the tube to his lips, his friend lifts the funnel, he drinks it fast, madness ensues.

Hair o' the Dog: Unavoidable consequence of this book. Enjoy!

Friendly Admonition

While drinking games stimulate your intellect, hone your wit like a sharpening stone, and may even inspire you to don a lampshade, they are also meant for a certain type of person: that person who knows and understands their own personal limits; and that person who, if it applies, plans ahead and arranges for a designated driver or a capable friend to make sure the passage home, whether by car, foot, or otherwise, is a safe one. Not only does the author implore you, but so does every stranger who shares the road with you and every loved one who shares a life with you; we all implore you to be that person. Such small efforts make everything a little better.

And here's where I gotta card you. Remember, in most places, twenty-one is the magic number!

50 Great College Drinking Games

1

KING TWO-BITS:

THE CLASSIC GAME OF QUARTERS AND ITS AGGRESSIVE OFFSPRING

The game of Quarters consists of bouncing a quarter into a cup. With nothing else to consider, it has become the undisputed king of drinking games. Great God . . . why?

What is so appealing about bouncing twenty-five cents into a cup? The laughable test of skill, maybe? The pleasing chime of a successfully sunken quarter? Let's be honest here: shooting quarters is not hard. After just a little practice you can get pretty good and start rockin' a table with ruthless precision by the influential flick of your wrist. But what's it worth? You can't shoot quarters in Vegas. You can't bring Quarters home to meet mom. And you certainly can't get a respectable job shooting quarters.

Well for starters, you can definitely get creative, and we all know how good that feels. Ordinarily, a quarter is shot by holding it between your thumb and forefinger and bouncing it flatly off the table and into the cup. This is the standard method and it works fairly well. Don't, however, be misled into thinking it's the only way to shoot a quarter. My brother was locally renowned for rolling the quarter off the casual curve of his Swedish nose, allowing it to bounce neatly on its rim, nine times out of ten right into the cup. Magic. He murdered us that way.

Still, why is Quarters #1? It could lie in the pressure-prone nature of a game like Speed Quarters. Some players *need* pressure and thrive off the tension of Speed Quarters, tauntingly waiting with cup and coin while the other cup zooms around the table. Then, at the last possible moment, they sink that shiny coin with grace, shamelessly burying their sorry neighbor to the sound of mocking guffaws all around.

Maybe it's just Drinking Game Darwinism! No, forget it. That idea struggles.

I suppose the explanation for the massive popularity of Quarters is ultimately elusive. But seeking the answer is a dumb-ass pursuit. In the end you'll have to explain why bouncing a quarter into a small cup is a feat of such remarkable skill that somebody should acknowledge it through the consumption of a beverage; *and* you'll have to explain why doing it three times in a row confers on the shooter the favored status of "table legislator." It's best just to play and forget about the rest.

I've arranged the game of Quarters and its derivatives in this chapter so as to follow a growing level of intensity. A group of party-goers, armed with a chilly case of Brown Derby beer and some tall St. Ides forties, may begin at Quarters feeling mildly competitive and only half interested in going crazy. However, by the time they've reached QP^2, someone better call Planter's because these folks will really be going nuts!

Quarters

Requirements:

- 1 quarter
- 1 coffee-sized cup
- a good, solid table that either doesn't scratch or you don't care if it does

Directions:

At the table, a player starts by attempting to bounce the quarter off the table and into the cup. If that person misses, he passes the quarter on to the next person. If she makes it, the player of her choice must recognize her accomplishment by sipping from his beverage. She then bounces again and does so until she misses. If a player makes three shots in a row, he or she can create a rule for the table (see Commentary). If the rule isn't followed, the perpetrator is penalized through enjoyment of a cool beverage.

Commentary:

Quarters is the Grand Poo-Bah of all drinking games. While being a great starter game for any party, Quarters also excels as a late night dynamo. The rules you can make after three in a row are as limitless as your own creativity. Some of the more well-known table rules are:

> • Thumbmaster: The rulemaker hangs his thumb on the table at any given time, and the last person to notice and then follow suit must drink.
> • No swearing
> • No first names
> • No saying the words "drink, drank, drunk"
> • If the quarter lands in the cup heads up, the person to the shooter's right must drink

These are just examples. My buddy Lee was one of the great Quarters legislators of all time. He'd have us calling each other different names and consuming full bottles when the phone rang. Often the best Quarters games are the ones with creative and difficult table rules.

Finally, knowing how to shoot a quarter is a good thing. If you get it down now, before you move on in the book, you'll be quite an ass-kicker in some of the later games. Don't get too good, though, or people will think you're a loser with nothing better to do. And they'll be right.

Speed Quarters

Requirements:

- 2 quarters
- 2 equal, coffee-sized cups
- same table as required for Quarters

Directions:

At the table, set the cups as far away as possible from one another. Like standard Quarters, you're trying to bounce a quarter into the cup in front of you. The difference is that once you sink your quarter, you must quickly pass the quarter *and* the cup to the anxious player to your left. He's anxious because the second cup is being passed around and the other players are shooting the other quarter into *it*. When that other cup gets to you, shoot *that* quarter into *that* cup. The object is to make the quarter into the cup before the other cup, making its way around the other side of the table, catches up to you. In the tragic event that, try as you might, you can't seem to sink your quarter into your cup and the other cup reaches you, the game pauses while you enjoy a drink. When you're finished, the game resumes.

Commentary:

Speed Quarters is the natural progression from standard Quarters into something that still tests your skill, but now tests it under duress. This game is a heap of fun when you have four or more people. If you don't have at least four, think twice. You'll be sorry otherwise.

Chandeliers

Requirements:

- X personal cups (X = the number of players in the game)
- 1 communal cup
- 1 quarter
- a solid table

Directions:

Place the communal cup in the middle and then closely surround it with the personal cups so they're all touching the communal cup. Each personal cup should correspond to a player. The communal cup should be filled to the rim with a beverage, while the smaller cups should be about one-fifth full. One by one, players attempt to shoot the quarter into either someone else's personal cup or into the communal cup.

Shooting the quarter into someone's personal cup requires the player assigned to that cup to drink its contents. However, if the quarter is shot into the communal cup, everyone must drink the contents of their personal cups as fast as possible.

The last player to finish his personal cup is disciplined for such embarrassingly sluggish consumption by having to exhaust the contents of the communal cup. As in basic Quarters, a player making three in a row can create a table rule.

Commentary:

A little thrill, a little punishment, a little spill on your collar: It's all part of this classic contest that probably stands as the most popular Quarters derivative in the chapter.

The thing I like the most about Chandeliers is, of all things, the name! Kudos to the drunkard who coined this gem, because enough of Chandeliers, this rollicking cousin to Quarters, and you'll be swinging from one. Enjoy!

Spin Quarters

Requirements:

- 1 quarter
- 1 shot glass
- 1 communal cup
- a solid table

Directions:

Fill up the communal cup about halfway with your favorite beverage. One person starts by shooting the quarter into the shot glass (you won't be using the shot glass for anything but shooting the quarter into it). If he makes it, he gives over to the player of his choice the quarter and the communal cup.

That chosen player then spins the quarter on its edge. While it spins, she must drink the contents of the communal cup. When finished, she taps the spinning quarter with the bottom of the cup. If the quarter stops on heads, she is done and the quarter returns to the player who was previously shooting into the shot glass, and he shoots until he misses. If it stops on tails, the poor soul must repeat the process until she gets a heads up.

One catch: if while the quarter is spinning, someone yells "Heads!" and the quarter stops on heads, the player must spin and drink again. But, if heads is called and it comes up tails, the gambler who incorrectly called "Heads!" must pay for his foolish prank by assuming the quarter, the cup, and the spin. As in basic Quarters, a player making three in a row can create a table rule.

Commentary:

Thanks to Spin Quarters and my accompanying stupidity, I lost a four dollar hamburger and some hot fries onto the pavement next to a Dumpster. You don't want that, so be especially aware of your limits. Spin Quarters, you see, compares to an exciting ride at the amusement park. It's got bounces and spins, taps and turns, twists and spills. But don't let those Tilt-A-Whirl adjectives throw you: Spin Quarters may seem like an innocent ride on the Zipper or the Pirate Ship, but play it long enough and you'll swear you bought a ticket for the toilet bowl Hurl-O-Rama. And OF COURSE that's funny for the rest of us, but wouldn't you rather we laugh *with* your clever wit and not *at* your sorry ass?

Anchor-Man

Requirements:

- 1 quarter
- 1 large pitcher or comparable container
- 2 small cups
- a solid table

Directions:

Divide the participants into two separate but equal teams. Place a full pitcher in the middle of the table and have each team sit on different sides of the table. Each team then chooses an Anchor-Man by shooting the quarter into the small cup. The last person to make it becomes the Anchor-Man for that team. Seating order is not important. When these details have been carried through, put the small cups away and take a deep breath. You are now ready to proceed with the slightly perverse game of Anchor-Man.

Flip the quarter to decide who will shoot first. Suppose Team A wins the toss. The first member of Team A bounces the quarter off the table, attempting to make it into the pitcher. If he misses, player one on Team B shoots. The quarter alternates from team to team until someone makes it into the pitcher. Let's say a player on Team A makes it. In response, Team B must drink the contents of the pitcher. Here's where the game gets ugly. Each of the players on the losing Team B *other than the Anchor-Man* can drink however much or however little they want. Whatever they don't drink, though, is left for the distressing Anchor-Man to consume. It is the responsibility of the Anchor-Man to see that not a single drop remains in the mighty pitcher at round's end.

Once the Anchor-Man has finished, pick a new anchor and play again.

Commentary:

If you're the Anchor-Man, pray hard that you're not Jesus on the Judas team. Your teammates, not unlike apostles, are supposed to like you and look out for you. As Anchor-Man, you have to hope they'll share the burden of the pitcher with you and not turn double-crosser by inhaling a traitor baby sip. It's a difficult lesson, but you do learn who your friends are.

The unspoken rule is that generally, being Anchor-Man is like having the chicken pox: you only get it once.

Game Day

Requirements:

- 1 pitcher
- 3 bottle caps
- a solid table

Directions:

The rules are similar to Anchor-Man. Players divide into two teams. Fill the pitcher to capacity and then float the three bottle caps on the surface, underside up. Now, lace up your cleats and get ready for Game Day, an American original.

The first player on Team A shoots the quarter, attempting to get it in the pitcher. If she misses, that counts as one out, and there are three outs per inning per team. If she makes it, she has scored a single and there's now a runner on first. (In recognition of the single, Team B players indulge momentarily in their beverages.) If she'd hit any one of the three floating bottle caps, that's an out-of-the-park, honest-to-goodness Hank Aaron style home run dong. All runners on base, if there are any, score, and Team B must drink the pitcher to completion. Enjoy!

Once Team A has three outs, Team B goes up to bat. Play as many innings as you like, but remember: the losing team must drink the pitcher.

Commentary:

Game Day is Anchor-Man times ten. Whether that's a good thing or not I'm not sure, but it is a hell of a game and much more exciting than watching whining millionaires play real baseball and fail to hit .400 for yet another year.

If you want to make the evening a double-header, finish up here and hit the diamond for a little Sloshball (see Chapter 5).

QP^2

Requirements:

- 1 quarter
- 2 pennies
- 3 cups
- a solid table

Directions:

The object here is the same as in Speed Quarters. You're racing to make your coin into the cup before the people to your right manage to make the coins they're shooting into their cups. The difference here is that the penalties are more severe and the pressure even more intense.

Set the three cups as far away from each other as possible on the table. Now, instead of dealing with two quarters, you're dealing with one quarter and two pennies. Whichever coin you might have, you shoot and try to make it into the cup that comes with the coin before getting caught by any of the other active coinage and their cups. When you make it, pass it all to the person on your left.

If a quarter catches a penny or a penny catches a quarter, you need only take a single swallow. As you enjoy your penalty swallow, the game continues around you, so you must enjoy it quickly. If a penny catches a penny, however, you've got problems. The game stops while you shotgun a full can or bottle of your favorite beverage. Once the can is empty, the game immediately resumes, hardly leaving you enough time to let out a much needed belch.

Commentary:

With high pressure, high intensity, maximum thrill, and a tremendous incentive to sink the coin into the cup, this game has all the makings of a blockbuster. QP^2 was conceived by me and some friends on the coveted "Day the Pipe Burst," when Speed Quarters simply couldn't satisfy our competitive spirits. So we dropped a quarter, added two pennies, made the penalties

more severe, and called it QP². Because of its
intensity and high penalization, I only recommend QP² to the experienced, rugged, and toler-
ant few.

2

DEALT A BRUTAL BLOW

GAMES INVOLVING THE ENIGMATIC DECK OF CARDS

Nobody knows the exact origin of the deck of cards. Its held by many scholars to have originated in China or Hindustan in about 800 A.D. Four hundred years later it was making its way around Europe, and by the late 1500s some crazy French person came up with the four suits, God knows how. Not much is known beyond this meager collection of information.

This spotty explanation disappoints me, because I'm not ashamed to say that I love cards. There is nothing so distinct as the deck of cards. Pick one up and ask yourself, what are the rules to this game? You won't find an answer. Unlike Monopoly, whose guidelines are set and whose purpose is obvious, the deck of cards has neither guidelines nor purpose until one is assigned to it. The king can hold your desire in one game and your dread in another. Such a transient approach to meaning gives the deck of cards immense diversity.

There remains a part of me, though, that craves an explanation. For instance, I always wanted to know who decided that the jack would be a member of the deck, and why. I wanted to know so badly that, for lack of one, I formulated my own origin theory. It goes like this:

Long ago there was a medieval village. While herding, the shepherds of this village developed a numbered deck of cards to pass the time between shearings. Life was serene, even though they lived under the dominion of the nefarious King and his oversexed and idiotic son, Prince Jack.

When the shepherds brought the cards back from the meadows, their popularity spread quickly, much like the curd had. But before long the King learned about the cards and demanded that they recognize the royal family. The shepherds complied, fearing for their lives, but the unlikable Prince would have to share his card with the hard-working mule. The head shepherd released a statement saying, "Indeed, the card honors our valiant Prince Jack, but it also honors our toiling mule, the ass." Eventually, the "ass" fell off the "jackass" card and left a card called the "jack," which the shepherd then said "may only be played when playing with thyself."

Amazing! In the same way, the whole deck of cards is open to that kind of interpretation. Without set rules, I could turn a ho-hum four of spades into the most desirable card in the deck.

The game, meant only for dudes, could be called "Heavy Metal Four," in which getting dealt the four of spades makes you the table's rock star and gets you all the chicks in fishnet stockings. That would turn the four-of-spades doldrums into its thrilling contrary. "Screw Prince Jack," you'd say with giddiness, "deal me the four and let's rock!" And since I am chasing arena rock stardom, Heavy Metal Four is my favorite game.

There's one aspect of drinking games with cards that doesn't change despite different games and rules: they can deal you a brutal blow. The best advice is to swamp your neighbor. Do it to her before she does it to you.

Up the River, Down the River

Requirements:

- • 1 deck of cards

Directions:

One player acts as the dealer and deals each player four cards. Each player displays their four cards faceup on the table. From the stack of undealt cards the dealer turns over one card at a time. You are recognizing two conditions in this game: either you're going Up the River or you're going Down the River. The two are defined as follows:

• **To go** *Up the River*: the dealer begins the game by going "Up the River." He turns a card over from the undealt deck and says, "Take *one*." This means that if the dealer turns over a queen, and one of your four cards is a queen, you must take one drink from your beverage. When all players who have queens have taken their drinks, the dealer turns over the next card and says, "Take *two*." If, for example, the card turned over is a deuce, and you have a deuce, you must take two drinks. This rationale continues in numerical order Up the River until the dealer ends at "Take *four*." Every game begins by going Up the River. After all required players have taken four drinks on "Take *four*," the dealer begins going Down the River.

• **To go** *Down the River*: the dealer turns a card over from the undealt deck and says, "Give *four*." If, for example, the card turned over is a seven and you have a seven, you can give four drinks to any player of your choice. After all drinks, the dealer turns over another card and says, "Give *three*." In like fashion, if you have the same card as the card turned over, you can give three drinks to another player. The dealer's numerical descent from "Give four" to "Give one" is called going "Down the River." After "give one" has been played, the dealer starts the numerical ascent back Up the River.

Commentary:

This is a classic card game known everywhere from Georgetown to Westwood. Up the River was a favorite of mine until, in a moment of humiliation rivaled only by being discovered by my older brother playing air guitar in front of the mirror to a Night Ranger album, I was nabbed cheating as the dealer. Holding the deck, I caught a glimpse of every card coming and could decide when I wanted to play that card. The others discovered this when one of the more alert participants noticed that I was eluding every bad card and embracing all the good ones.

I know, I know: cheating at drinking games, how pathetic. Air-guitaring to "Sister Christian" has more charm.

Blind Man's Bullshit

Requirements:

- 1 deck of cards

Directions:

This game is similar to Up the River, Down the River, in that each player is dealt four cards. However, three major things are different. First, the four cards remain facedown in front of the player. Second, each player may look at his cards only once before turning them facedown. He must try to remember not only which cards he has, but in which order he has them arranged in front of him.

Third, instead of a dealer drawing from a deck and going Up the River and then Down the River, the cards are laid out in the shape of a pyramid on the table:

Figure 1

Give One	
Give Two	
Give Three	
Give Four	
Give Five	
Give Six	

One by one and starting from the left end of the top row, the dealer turns over the cards. Remember that row number equals number of drinks. At each card a player can ask another player to drink. For example: a king comes up in the third row, and Player A asks Player B to take three drinks. Player B has two options: he may simply take the three drinks and go on with the game, or he may challenge Player A by demanding to see the king Player A claims to have.

Since the cards are facedown, Player A must go by memory in order to find the alleged king. Player B asserts this challenge by saying to Player A, "Bullshit!" Player A must locate his king on the first guess from the four cards facedown in front of him. If he does, Player B not only must enjoy the three drinks, but as a penalty for calling "Bullshit!" and being wrong, he must have yet another three. On the other hand, if Player A can't locate the king on the first guess, Player A must enjoy the three drinks which he meant for Player B.

Commentary:

Blind Man's Bullshit is to Up the River, Down the River, what QP^2 is to Speed Quarters: a notch up on intensity. I strongly encourage the ultralightweights to read on and discover some of the other card-playing gems that await you just beyond this powerhouse.

A common alias is Pyramid of Death, which, while very accurate, is not as popular. But you can call it Jai Alai or Judas Priest or Fresh Donuts if you want, because it just doesn't matter. Enjoy!

Asshole

Requirements:

- 1 deck of cards

Directions:

The true object of the great game of Asshole is, essentially, not to be one. This proves more difficult for some than it does for others.

Sit in a circle and deal the cards to each player until all the cards are *evenly* distributed. For example, if you have five players, deal ten cards per player and set aside the remaining two cards.

The game's objective is to be the first to empty all the cards from your hand. The turn goes around the circle and each player lays down a card in the middle of the table. In order to lay down a card you must either match or beat the card played by the player before you. You beat a card by placing a higher denomination on top of it. You may also match it by playing the same card. Matching the card gets a card out of your hand and it also skips your neighbor's turn. If you don't have a card that is playable to the above standards, you must pass on your turn.

The only all-powerful card in the deck is the deuce. It can be played in turn at any time, regardless of what's on top of the pile. When the deuce is played, the pile is cleared and the player of the deuce can set down a new card.

If you have doubles or triples of a particular card in your hand, you can lay them all down in the same turn at the same time. You may only do so, however, if you have played a deuce and are starting a new pile. It's a good move, especially since the next player must also play doubles or triples equal to or higher than yours to get to play at all. If he doesn't have it, he must pass. The next player must play off the pile if he can. He does not start a new one simply because the previous player has passed.

The order of people emptying their hands builds a hierarchy for the next game. The first person to have played all their cards is called the King and the last player left with cards in hand is called the Asshole.

Once the hierarchy is set, you play another round. The difference with this next round is that there's an Asshole at the table (depending on who's playing, that may not prove to make much of a difference). He becomes everyone's whipping boy; anyone can ask anything of him. The King, by virtue of his superior performance, may ask anything of anyone. In other words, if the King wants another beverage from the fridge or if he would like someone to scratch his back, he can direct that request to anyone at the table, confident his request will be fulfilled. Accordingly, the Queen, the second player to empty his hand, may ask anything of anyone except the King, and so on.

Now, in addition to *being* an Asshole, it is the responsibility of the Asshole to keep a running count of how many deuces have been played, since that knowledge can factor into your strategy. A typical dialogue concerning the deuces would be as follows:

Queen: Asshole, how many deuces have been played?
Asshole: Um, gosh, ma'am, I . . . well, two maybe. Or three.
Queen: What a disgrace! Finish your beverage.
Asshole: But . . .
Queen: Finish your beverage, you sorry asshole!

The seating for the next round should reflect the hierarchy, so that the King is at the head of the table and the Asshole is sitting in a high-chair or something comparably humiliating. Don't feel pity for the Asshole; he can only be punished for his pathetic performance through group ridicule.

Commentary:

There are few games with as much class distinction, outright snobbery, flagrant abuse of power, inhuman treatment, and the kind of belittling degradation that feels so damn good to deliver.

The game's most notable alias is "Mr. President," a name which manages to be a little more safe and a little less offensive.

Horse Races

Requirements:

- 1 deck of cards

Directions:

Designate a dealer, who will then pull the aces from the deck and line them face up in front of her. She then places six random cards in a line on her right-hand side, all going perpendicular to the aces. It does not matter if they are face up or face down.

Each player will now bet on a particular ace. The wager is always the same: Lose - take a drink. Win - do not take a drink. The dealer then turns over one card at a time from the deck. Whatever suit the card is, the ace of the same suit will advance upward, one card length at a time (this length is measured by the rows of

cards to the right of the dealer). The hope is that
the ace upon which you wagered reaches the
sixth card first. If so, you win! And you watch all
the losers drink. If not . . . you are one of the
losers. Don't let it upset you.

Commentary:

I can't help but think of the carnival game where
you shoot water into the mouth of a clown's head
in order to fill up a balloon, or see your plastic
camel bob up and down into first place. In that
case, your prize is a cheap, stuffed Panda bear or
a mirror with an acid-etched Harley-Davidson
decal. Depending on what you're into, these
prizes may be pretty damn valuable!

This game crawled out of infamous Chico,
California; a place where, it's estimated, a person can always find at least one drinking game
going down at any minute of the day. That
amounts to nothing short of a Mecca for some of
you hard-core, indulgent players; but don't you
have something better to do?

King's Cup

Requirements:

- face cards, aces, deuces, tens from one deck
- 1 communal cup (the "King's cup")
- your thinking cap

Directions:

Place the empty King's cup at the center of the table. Shuffle the twenty-four necessary cards and scatter them facedown around the King's cup. Each player, in turn, will flip over a card. The cards have the following meanings:

- Ace – social drink
- King – The first three kings turned over mean only that the player who draws them must add beverage to the King's cup. She can add as much or as little as she likes. The fourth king, however, requires the guilty player to exhaust the contents of the King's cup. When that occurs, the game begins again.
- Queen – person to the active player's right drinks
- Jack – person to the active player's left drinks
- Ten and deuce – These are "category" cards. The player who turns over a ten or a deuce chooses a category at random. For example, she may choose Kevin Costner movies. She then must name a Costner flick (*Sizzle Beach, USA* counts, although maybe not to Kevin). The category circles the table until it gets to someone who can't think of a film with Costner in it. That person, obviously not wearing his thinking cap, must pay for his forgetfulness by enjoying a healthy gulp.

Commentary:

I played the finest game of King's Cup while
camping at Big Sur in California one summer.
Out under the moonlight next to a crackling fire,
my friend Dave and I smoked Nat Shermans and
drank Natural Light while coming up with some
classic categories, the most outstanding being
"Rockers from Our High School," among which
we proudly included ourselves.

King's Cup can mellow out a party in no time.
For that reason, it's a game to be played as either
a starter for a calm party or as a late night wash.
The consumption is fairly heavy despite its relaxed
and cognitive aura, especially if you're the dismal
flop who keeps turning over the last king. Still, the
categories are always fun, and you might surprise
yourself as to how many Kiss albums you can
remember.

Cops and Pushers

Requirements:

- 1 ace
- 1 king
- X minus two cards (other than face cards and
  aces)

Directions:

Mix up the cards and lay them facedown on the table. Each player discreetly chooses a card, making absolutely sure that nobody else sees it, including the family cat or the whistling canary: In Cops and Pushers you can trust no one.

The player who has drawn the ace is the pusher. The player who has drawn the king is the cop. Everyone else is a potential buyer. What transpires then is: the pusher's looking for someone to buy his product, but in order to do so, he must make a deal. To make a deal, the pusher covertly flashes a quick, nonchalant wink to any one of the other players, taking his sweet time, trying his damnedest to make sure no one else saw this transaction. Once the wink has been executed, the player on the receiving end waits a moment or two and then says:

"The deal has been made."

She then turns over her card. It's now up to the cop, the player with the king, to figure out the identity of the pusher.

The cop reveals his own identity by showing everyone his king. He then sets out to capture the culprit. If the cop played it right, he saw the transaction go down when it did and he wastes no time in pointing out the pusher. If the cop is correct on the first guess, the indolent pusher must do hard time drinking his full beverage into depletion. But if the cop is wrong, he drinks. If on his second guess he's wrong again, he drinks more. Wrong again? The shame of it all! He drinks even more. If he can't guess correctly, forget it. Take his badge away, call him a disgrace if you must, and make him pound a full beverage or take a visit to the shot glass.

If the pusher has the misfortune to make the deal with the cop, he suffers the customary punitive fate of slamming a full one. But c'mon . . . nobody's *that* stupid.

Commentary:

A classic game, but be sure to keep a brisk pace through each round. Otherwise the game drags on and on, and pretty soon the group will have collapsed into factions who are too busy yapping in belligerence to pay any attention to the game. While this is symptomatic of all drinking games, it is especially true for this one.

A.k.a. Cops and Robbers, a.k.a. FBI's Most Wanted. Call it what you will, this headbanger still packs the same treacherous punch.

Suck and Blow

Requirements:

- all cards from any one suit

Directions:

Begin with the deuce. One player puts the card up to his lips and creates a suction so that the card is suspended face out from his mouth. The player to his left must then lean in and begin sucking at the card. While the second player sucks, the first player must blow. The object is to pass the card between two people by using only the powers of the lips and lungs. Once the deuce has made its way around the table, you move on to the three, and so on. If two players drop a card, they must drink according to the value of the card. In other words, if the players drop a six, they must suck up six swallows from their beverage, and try at the six again.

Commentary:

Seating arrangement is paramount in Suck and Blow. Try to be sure your neighbors are people you don't mind kissing because, well, I won't lie to you, it does happen. Be ready for the token homophobic/latent homosexual to say, "Boy girl, man. We sit boy fuckin' girl or I ain't playin'!"

You drink more than you might want in this game, too. Dropping the jack or the queen sucks, excuse the pun, because that's an awful lot of beverage to take down. In addition, after taking ten or eleven drinks, you have to try to pass the card again. It's doubtful the card will remain sucked to your lips when you roar the hefty belch brewing in your nucleus. Nor will your partner be too happy about that hoppy burst of humid stench. But while burping is considered offensive and not socially acceptable, you gotta do it, so go right ahead and relieve yourself of that inner bubble. It's gonna feel super if you do, and I think I know you well enough by now to say, "Hey, let it all out."

Spoons

Requirements:

- one less spoon than X
- sets of four-of-a kind cards equal to X

Directions:

Spread out the spoons evenly in the middle of the table and then deal four random cards to each player. What players are trying to accomplish is to gather four of a kind before anyone else can achieve that same goal. Players look at their cards and try to determine which card to throw out. On a three count, players place the unwanted card facedown next to the player to their right, who looks at it and decides if she wants it. This process is repeated swiftly. The first person to have four of a kind reaches out and takes a spoon. When the other players see that, they must scramble for the remaining spoons. The player who does not get a spoon, but has no doubt earned scratches and scrapes in the scramble, must drink substantially before the next round begins.

Commentary:

Spoons goes back many years. My mother remembers it, but she doesn't remember drinking being the penalty . . . clearly a recent, more beneficial adaptation. My ex-girlfriend's family adored this game, playing late into the night through Marlboro smoke and tall shots of Stoli, diving over the table, knocking down chairs and wrestling spoons from each other's hands with desperation and deep-seeded hostility and aggression, all in the name of good family fun.

Suck the Sock

Requirements:

- 1 clean sock
- 1 joker (and I don't mean you, crazy nut!)
- remaining face cards, aces, deuces, tens

Directions:

Separate the joker from the rest of the cards. Now combine the joker with as many cards as needed to give every player a single card and deal them out, leaving the deck in a central location.

Each player looks at his card. One by one and to the left, players turn over a card from the central deck. If it is not the ace of spades, all players pass their card to the right and adhere to the meanings listed below. If it *is* the ace of spades, the unluckiest of all drinking game players is the one with the joker, who must drape the sock over his beverage. Each time during the next round that the game calls on him to drink, he must do so through the sock.

All the other cards have the following meanings throughout the course of the game:

- Ace (other than the ace of spades) – switch direction in passing the cards
- King – player chooses another to drink
- Queen – person to the active player's right drinks
- Jack – person to the active player's left drinks
- Ten – player who draws a ten must drink
- Deuce – category cards. The player who turns over a ten or a deuce chooses a category at random. Remember this from King's Cup? If not, seek out your answer there.

Commentary:

This game is just a baby, conceived in the winter of 1995, but I can already see that it will someday become a national sensation. During this game's exciting formation, it was suggested that instead of passing around the same sock, players should use one off their own feet. Not surprisingly, this experiment proved disastrous and is not recommended.

In placing the sock over the bottle, you can't help but be reminded of the Red Hot Chili Peppers' tube sock days, which no doubt invites phallic comparisons ranging from oral sex to the application of a condom to the universal male tradition of masturbating into a gym sock. These analogies are nothing but a smear campaign to stop the already mounting popularity of this dynamo, so I don't give in to them. Once you've sat a spell at the Suck the Sock table, you'll see why this powerhouse is rockin' the very foundations of the establishment.

3

CASTING THE DIE

GAMES INVOLVING DICE

You can't predict the roll of the die. You might think you have an idea about what it might be depending on what happened before and what might happen afterward, but what happens in between is not a matter of mathematics but of chance. For that reason, I find myself liking dice games more and more, and liking other people who like dice games more and more as well. Gamblers, bettors, crapshooters, people who like to do the itchy-scratchy with lady luck, all share a deep bond and a strange fascination with the timeless roll of the bones.

Classic games like Three-Man challenge one's love for the dice. You can become the Three-Man not because you're a bastard child or because you pissed your bed, but because you said you'd play. Skills hit the trash can and you welcome unpredictability. Fortunately for us in the lower income bracket, only sobriety is at stake, and not a humble nest egg.

Still, that can prove to be quite a gamble.

Consider Live Wire: it's you versus an opponent in a high-voltage race against time and the odds. Or Beer Die, a total original, where you must finesse nature's laws, play catch, pray for a good roll, *and* conform to the rules of Buzz (Chapter 4). And that's just to escape a whipping. You'll also discover 7–14–21 and Mexicali here, the latter practically a barroom pastime.

So play dice games with heart, but don't barter your soul. Don't fool yourself into thinking that blowing your bad breath on the dice or shaking them like a mariachi is really going to help you. Dice, like cats, don't give a piece of pie what ritual you perform, because in the end they're gonna do what they want anyway. It's like putting a student on the University Board of Regents. He or she may have a say, but no one on the board is listening. In this respect, dice can do whatever they want. If only they could dress me in spandex and make me a rock star!

Three-Man

Requirements:

- 1 hat or cap, preferably silly-looking
- 1 pair of dice

Directions:

A "Three-Man" is simply a person who must don
a silly hat and drink every time a three is rolled.
Each player rolls one die to determine the game's
initial Three-Man. He or she with the lowest roll is
awarded the status of Three-Man, cap included.
Tough shit if the cap messes up your hair.

There is only one Three-Man per table at a
time, and the only way the Three-Man can relin-
quish his "reign" is to roll a three when it's his
turn. If he does, he may give over the Three-Man
cap to any player he chooses. The other players
roll when it's their turn, giving and taking drinks
according to the following table:

Figure 2

Roller gives out one drink.

Three-Man drinks; roller gives out one die for
any player to roll and outcome is quantity
necessary to drink.

Three-Man drinks; social drink (everyone).

Each player must put right index finger to
right side of nose. Last player to do so must
drink.

Nothing (unless you have a No-Man, in
which case he drinks). Player loses turn.

Nothing (see 1 & 5). Player loses turn.

Roller gives out two drinks.

Three-Man drinks.

Nothing.

"Seven to the right" means player to the shooter's right drinks.

Nothing.

Three-Man drinks, roller gives out three.

Three-Man drinks, "Seven to the right."

Three-Man drinks.

Three-Man drinks.

Roller gives out four drinks.

Nothing.

Nothing.

Roller gives out five drinks.

"Eleven to the left" means the player to the roller's left drinks.

Roller gives out six drinks.

Commentary:

This game has such a tremendous following that a Three-Man has emerged as something of a metaphor in the English language. While its final definition wholly evades us, steeped in the mechanics of chance and destiny, we can find some understanding of what it means to be the Three-Man if we apply it to our practical lives:

Three-Man (thre/man), *n, pl* **-Men**, *v.*, **-Manned**, **-Manhandled** *(var)*, **-Maneuvered** *(var)* **1**. one whose existence is temporarily screwed over, thanks to fate or otherwise **2**. a Christlike figure, Promethean in stature, Ahabesque in passion, whose role is to suffer the slings and arrows of the tumble of the dice **3**. the grim reaper of the practical, drinking world: *Derek's day was doomed from the start with a visit from the Three-Man, who first stalled his car on the bridge and then whispered nasties into his ear, which he repeated in a blank, glossy stare to his boss.* **4**. a position you should avoid ~*vt* **1**. to find one's self getting raked over through no particular fault of one's own, as though someone high up decided they despised you and that was that: *Egad! How could I have been Three-Manned even though I paid my taxes and volunteered at the Y!?*

Beer Die

Requirements:

- 4 tumbler-sized cups
- 2 coffee-sized cups
- a long table (about 8 x 3 feet)
- 1 die
- 2 similar, sturdy chairs

Directions:

Two players compete at a time, both armed with a single coffee cup. And don't forget to buckle up; this one's a bitch.

Agree on a point goal to determine a winner. Then fill the four cups to near capacity and put them at the four corners of the table. Place the two chairs about four feet from each end of the table and turn them backward. Now, players will balance themselves on the back of the chair, facing the table. This, believe it or not, is your playing field.

The first player will lob the die in the air, aiming somewhere in the middle of the table in an attempt to bounce it into one of his opponent's cups. That's the central object: to sink the die, off one bounce, into the cups on your opponent's side. Do this and you score three points, and she must drink the cup to completion. She then spits the die out onto the table. If the roll shows a three or a five, she must do it again. However, the words "three" and "five" can not be uttered at any time during the course of the game. Instead, one must use "bizz" for *three* and "buzz" for *five*. An example follows:

"Heh, what time is it?"
"It's twenty-buzz to bizz."
"Okay. Thanks, you sorry asshole!" (Oops, wrong game!)

Failure to adhere to this results in—you guessed it, hijos . . . drink up.

There are other ways to score. A point is awarded when your opponent misses your cups but you deftly catch the dice in your coffee cup on the way to the floor. If you merely *hit* your opponent's cup with the dice, score yourself a point. You lose a point if your shot does not stay in the fair playing area, but bounces off the table widthwise. Remember that, like all drinking games, scoring a point in any fashion earns your opponent the customary penalty.

Commentary:

This powerhouse originated at Colby College in Waterville, Maine. According to local legend, in the late 1980s, after Colby banned kegs from the dorms, the game became so popular that all the folding tables had to be chained to walls, pipes, etc., to prevent their disappearance from study halls and sudden reemergence at the clandestine, movable feasts where Beer Die reigned.

And once again, the near-fabled mystique of the early to mid-eighties rears its head. The reaction to John Belushi-inspired nights of dementia has left a legacy of moderation devastating enough to make possible the advent of a game like Beer Die nowadays very scarce. However, ideologies, like bell bottoms and lucky Lazarus, tend to make comebacks, so keep your eyes peeled.

Note: Maine locals, perhaps just a bit too close to the magnetic pole for clear thinking, refer to their post–Beer Die inebriation as "wicked shitty." So despite its unappetizing ring, please refer to this at least once out of respect for this explosive contest and the courageous students who hatched it for you.

Mexicali

Requirements:

- 1 Yahtzee-style cup (not see-through)
- 1 set of dice

Directions:

A person begins by rolling the dice in the cup, looking at the outcome, then telling the person to their left what they have. The roller can tell the truth about the roll or she can lie.

The next person must decide if they think the roller is lying or not. If that next player says,

"You're lying. Show me your double threes," and
she indeed has double threes, he must drink and
his turn is skipped. However, the double threes
now move on to challenge the next player. If he
decides to accept the double threes as true, he
rolls the dice in the cup. What he's trying to do is
garner a roll that has a higher value than the roll
confronting him, in this case the double threes.
Mexicali values are as follows:

Figure 3

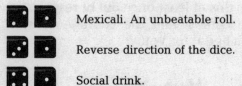

Mexicali. An unbeatable roll.

Reverse direction of the dice.

Social drink.

Always count a roll from high dice to low dice. In
other words, you will never score a 34. It will
always be a 43.

The point of each successive player is to claim
that their roll is higher than the previous roll, so
that the dice can make it back to them and
nobody will have been able to beat their score. If
this becomes the case, everyone drinks, minus
the player with the high roll.

Commentary:

A tricky move, making a drinking game where

success is contingent upon cerebral strategy, but Mexicali emerges with flying colors. Something to remember, though, is that four players proves ideal; five works okay, but any more than that and the game drags along like those endless Pearl Jam guitar solos, frivolous Oasis interviews, or oh, Jesus, another Stones album?

Live Wire

Requirements:

- 1 communal cup
- 1 pair of dice

Directions:

Fill the cup to the rim with your most exciting beverage. One person begins by rolling the dice. If she rolls a seven, an eleven, or doubles, she may choose one player at the table. He, the chosen participant, must now drink the contents of the communal cup. While he drinks, the roller is throwing the dice over and over trying to roll a seven, an eleven, or doubles before the chosen drinker can finish the beverage. He wants to finish the drink before the roller is able to roll one of the mentioned combinations. If he can, he's the lucky recipient of the dice. If not, sorry! Refill the cup. She rolls, he drinks again, until he can finish before she can.

Commentary:

The name surely fits the game, folks. This bastard is electric. This battle has been known by the following *alias très tedious*: 7–11-Doubles. But I beseech you folks to drop that fatuous mess of numbers and letters and adopt the more appropriate "Live Wire," a name borrowed from an old Motley Crue tune, if we can believe the story from an all too often inebriated student out of Sonoma State in California.

Greg's Grog Game

Requirements:

- one die

Directions:

Simple simple simple. Roll the dice. The values have the following meanings:

1 – Take one drink
2 – Take two drinks
3 – Choose someone to take three drinks
4 – *Go to the bathroom*
5 – Person to the roller's left drinks
6 – Person to the roller's right drinks

If you do not roll a four, you cannot go to the bathroom. If you roll a four but you don't need to go, you may *not* cash it in later. Nor can you pass your four on to a more desperate player.

Commentary:

Perhaps a more suitable name for this contest might be Greg's Colostomy Bag Game.

I don't know where it came from or who Greg is, but I do know of some upstate New York and Washington, D.C. area bars that used to charge a reasonable cover when you walked in, and from then on all drinks were a nickel until the first person broke down and went to the bathroom. A good idea would be to see if you can work the idea of "holding it in" into some of the other games in the book. For instance, it could make a great rule for Quarters.

7-14-21

Requirements:

- 1 die

Directions:

This one is simple, but for the bar and not for the home. So hit an ATM for the eighty bucks it takes to enjoy yourself at a cheap bar these days and roll on out.

The first person rolls the single die, remembers her amount, and passes it on to the next person. The die goes round and round until one player's die rolls a total of seven points. That person decides on a drink from the bar. Now clear all scores and begin rolling again. The first unlucky player to fourteen has to buy the drink. Clear them all again. The unluckiest of all players will be the one to twenty-one, who has to consume the much-discussed drink.

Commentary:

This game often embodies that age-old adage, "What goes around, comes around." There's always some fool who thinks he's funny when he reaches fourteen and picks one of those wacky bar drinks with the wackier names and the even wackier ingredients. Naturally, he's the one wincing as he hits twenty-one first and shoots that not-so-funny-anymore prank down his throat. Come to think of it, there's always one fool in every drinking game. Why do you suppose that is? Do they, like county fairs and Ted Nugent gigs, just *attract* fools?

4

No Assembly Required

Games that Require No Outside Objects

Let me be the first to tell you how sweet it is, playing a game that could have been played by Neanderthals gathered around a sparkling campfire with handwoven baskets of wicked brew and slabs of meat on long sticks to keep their bellies full. You feel as though industrial society, the information age even, has taken a lunch break. Communication is not through e-mail, fax, or phone, but through a sign, a grunt, or majestic horns; something your prehistoric brother or sister may have cave-painted in southern France. Our heavy reliance on external things has lifted us off the dirt and on to a fluff that doesn't allow us to get in touch with our baser instincts. The games in this chapter, however, may offer you a glimpse. No props here, folks. Just raw *you*, expressing your bad, bad self.

Thumper is by far the most notable metal-head in this chapter, and for good reason. But don't let it detract you from some of the other

gems. The sheer power and charm of Cardinal
Puff, for example, has earned a cult status for
this master. The Insult Game, while fairly
obscure, is louder and more abrasive than a
Lyndon Larouche rally. And Zoom Schwartz
Now, while quite possibly the most inane game
in the chapter, stands as one of the fastest and
one of the best in the book.

The main theme of this chapter, if it could be
said to have one, is absurdity. Don't bother
turning to this section until the wheels are
pretty slick. If you start out here, each game
will undoubtedly prove to be a real dud, elicit-
ing a three-word response from your guests as
they pinch their noses and sneer: "Oooh. This
one stinks." You'll be unpopular, your party
will fizzle like a bad joke, and people will see
you as a pathetic failure. But good God, these
games don't stink! You merely need to obey
the sense of drinking-game timing that's been
developing since you opened this book. Folks,
playing Thumper at the outset of your gather-
ing is like premature ejaculation: it makes
no one happy. But play these monsters at the
right time—and only you know when that is—
and they won't disappoint you. For such simple
discretion, you'll be carried to the table triumph-
antly on the shoulders of your guests, which
sure beats being dragged to the lawn and
caned unmercifully across your tender, bare
cheeks.

Thumper

Requirements:

- less than zero

Directions:

Each player chooses a sign that can be made with the fingers, hands, lips, teeth, etc., like a peace sign or a salute or a brushing-your-teeth charade.

Once each player has chosen his sign, do a "sign check," which simply means that, going around the table, each player does her sign so that everyone can learn everyone else's. Once all signs are mastered, you're ready to begin Thumper, a true classic. It's a brisk one, so get a good solid grip on the safety bar.

All players aggressively beat their palms on the kitchen table. One player shouts with zeal, "What's the name of the game?"

The other players respond at the tops of their lungs, "THUMPER!"

First player yells, "How do you play?"

The other players respond by pounding their fists in unison to the words that they are yelling: "THUMP! . . . LIKE! . . . SHIT!"

Silence prevails. One designated player—the player who led the opening call and response—begins by acting out her sign, followed immediately by someone else's sign.

When that someone else sees his sign, he must do his sign and then someone else's. The game proceeds at a breakneck, roller rink speed until someone fouls up, which usually entails a panic-stricken participant charading an outlandish version of their own sign followed by an unidentifiable sign. That excited player drinks for his folly and begins the next round first by leading the group through the call and response and then beginning the game.

Commentary:

Now remember what I told you: Thumper relies on nonsense, so it's usually best to play it after a few other games have dampened your discretion and heightened your sensitivity *to* and appreciation *of* the absurd. And also, the more creative, offensive, or lewd your sign (there's always someone doing the oral sex thing), the better your game. Take a moment while coming up with your sign to ditch conventional ideas, since they have a way of butchering an otherwise sporting contest.

Several variations exist for the game's opening chant, the most common one ending in, "Get . . . fucked . . . up!" In addition, some people continue to beat their palms on the table while the signs are flashed. However, if you have the coordination to maintain that, maybe you should hold off playing Thumper until a little later in the evening, when your motor skills are a bit more shot.

Viking

Requirements:

- kinship to the mighty Nords

Directions:

One player begins as the Viking, using her hands on either side of her head to simulate horns. The player to the left of the Viking must simulate rowing with oars, as must the player to the right. However, each player on the side of the Viking must row specifically to his side. For instance, the player to the Viking's right must row with their left hand on top of their right and pull the invisible oar only to the right. This way, he compliments the oarsman to the Viking's left, and the robust Nord will sail a straight and sturdy course.

During all this, the Viking and her oarspeople must maintain the chant:

"I am a Viking going out to war. I am a Viking out to drink more."

When the Viking wishes to transfer the status to another player, she merely turns her head and horns in that person's direction. The chosen person assumes the horns, and the players to the right and left begin rowing. Any mistakes, naturally, mean a visit to the drinking horn.

Commentary:

Like Thumper, Viking is a rotten game if you play it first. Save it for later in the evening, when pretending to be a hearty Norwegian with horns is actually *funny*, and not stupid. Discovered while in the southern United States, Viking is so unbelievably inane that you find yourself hoping that whatever sod made up this game couldn't remember doing so the night before.

Zoom Schwartz Ñow

Requirements:

- a bono vox

Directions:

This is a face-to-face square-off, where two players are yelling one of the three words that are the title to this game at each other in order to fool the opponent. It may seem confusing, but there is nothing else to the game, and as few as three or as many as fifty can play at once. Best to define the three words first.

> **Zoom:** To "zoom" a competitor (to yell at someone "Zoom!") is to invite her into a challenge. What challenge? To fool each other into screwing up. Each round begins

with a "zoom." When Player A and Player B are engaged in a challenge, and Player A suddenly zooms Player C, Player B is free of the challenge. A "zoom" can be answered with a "schwartz" or a "ñow," but a player cannot immediately zoom the player who just zoomed them.

Schwartz: Said directly to the player's face quickly and without facial expression. To schwartz your opponent is to delay making a more substantial move, like zooming someone else or ñowing them. A schwartz can be answered with a ñow or another schwartz, but not with a zoom. Why? Because a zoom invites the challenge between two people. From then on, the two players can only say "schwartz" or "ñow" to one another.

Ñow: (Pronounced like the English "now" except the *n* is pronounced like the first *n* in the Spanish *mañana*.) A head fake to fool your competitor into thinking you're zooming someone. Why is this? Because, in this game, if you turn your head away, your opponent might think you're zooming someone else, and he may not respond, earning him a drink. You may not say "ñow" while looking at the person anyway. Doing that results in a loss and a drink.

Note: Skilled players employ the Doppler effect when saying "ñow."

Understand the terms? Good. As an example, this is how a game with three players moves:

> **Player A:** (to C) Zoom!
> **Player C:** (to A) Schwartz!
> **Player A:** Schwartz!
> **Player C:** (snapping her head) Ñow!
> **Player A:** (to B) Zoom!
> **Player B:** (to A in a panic) Um, zoom!?

See how Player B lost? This player also could have lost if she had mistaken a schwartz for a ñow and head-faked a schwartz to Player C. All schwartzes are to be directed to your opponent, as are all zooms. Ñows should be directed away from your opponent.

The loser drinks and begins the next round by zooming someone.

Commentary:

It seems confusing, but only on paper. Zoom Schwartz Ñow is a hell of a game and truly worth taking the few moments to learn. There were two people in my circle of drinking friends who considered Zoom . . . the finest of them all. While I wouldn't go that far, since there are no musical references, I will say that it does encompass many of the factors necessary for a classic:

absurdity, obnoxious confrontation, and a set of rules so unique that its tradition goes way back and will undoubtedly outlast your own drinking days.

Buzz

Requirements:

• what's left of your thinking cap

Directions:

Sit in a circle. One player begins by saying the number one. One by one and counting to the left, each player says the next number, and says it quickly. However, each time a seven is present or the number is divisible by seven, that player must simply say "buzz" in place of the number. In the event of error, the blunderer acknowledges, with a drink from a beverage, his inability to function in simple arithmetic.

Commentary:

Buzz's only recognized alias is Seven Seven Seven, although I recommend using Buzz, with a nod to Beer Die in Chapter 3.

Unlike most of the games in this chapter, Buzz can really work at the start of a party. Just remember that players must count quickly.

Giving everyone ample time to do the math is the best way to spoil this game.

So enough of Buzz, this deceptively trivial game of vocalized enumeration, and you'll be sure to have a good one!

Wanna Buy a Beer?

Requirements:

- duh . . .

Directions:

Two players compete at a time. The game consists of a dialogue spoken between them. It goes as follows:

Player 1: Wanna buy a beer?
Player 2: A what?
Player 1: A beer.
Player 2: Is it cold?
Player 1: Of course it's cold.

Once the two players have completed the dialogue, they must repeat it again and again. Here's the trick, though: the second time around, each line of dialogue must be spoken twice, as follows:

Player 1: Wanna buy a beer?
Player 2: Wanna buy a beer?

Player 1: A what?
Player 2: A what?
Player 1: A beer . . . etc.

The third time as follows:

Player 1: Wanna buy a beer?
Player 2: Wanna buy a beer?
Player 1: Wanna buy a beer?
Player 2: A what?
Player 1: A what?
Player 2: A what?
Player 1: A beer . . . etc.

The game continues until one of the players loses count and bungles it all up.

Commentary:

This rousing party pleaser has one catch: You gotta play it quick. Responses have to be so tight that they clip one another; otherwise this contest will dud like a disappointing firecracker or yet another Who reunion.

One Up, One Down
(When I Go Camping . . .)

Requirements:

- nothing

Directions:

This is the kind of game where only you and maybe one or two other people can know the rules. If everyone knows how to play . . . well then, forget it.

Okay, let's say you've said to your friends, "Heh, let's play 'One Up, One Down' tonight. It'll be a scream." They agree with apprehension, asking, "How do you play?" You ignore them and begin the game. You're sitting at the table with both elbows on the tabletop. You begin by saying, "Two up." The person to your left doesn't get it. So he drinks. The next person doesn't get it either. She drinks. The next does, however, and finds herself with one elbow on the table. She says, without shifting, "One up, one down." She may even then lift her elbow off the table and say casually, "Two down," before her turn is over, to help cue in a few of the slower members of the party. While thoughtful, it generally doesn't help.

Each time a person has yet to get it, he drinks. Once everyone gets it, you've killed the game and you'll need to move on. There's always one boob, though, at every table, who just can't get it. Be sure to get in as many laughs as you can at his expense.

Commentary:

"When I Go Camping," out of Oregon, is similar enough for me to add it here rather than claim it as an independent game. In "When . . ." the first player, whose name is let's say Ozzy, starts by saying, "When I go camping, I always bring my oval-shaped oranges." The next person doesn't get it. He drinks. The next person, however, does. Her name's Joan Jett. She says, "When I go camping, I always bring my jade-colored jammies." In other words, our in-house rock star has-beens are simply using the first letter of their first name. Play until everyone gets it. Again, be prepared for the crank who doesn't get it, even after "Weird Al" Yankovic has his turn.

Cricket

Requirements:

- a desire, even a tiny one, to learn some aspects of this bourgeois British sport

Directions:

Sit in a circle and remember that temporarily the
numbers four, six, and all their multiples are of
the utmost importance.

A player begins the game by pretending to
swing a cricket bat. If you don't know how, do
your best Ken Griffey, Jr. and call it Cricket. The
next player does the same. So does the next
player. The fourth player, instead of swinging a
bat, must act out the sign that a Cricket referee
makes when a player hits a four-run hit. What's
that sign, you ask? Sweep your right arm in front
of you as though you were clearing off a desk in
one swoop, meanwhile wiggling your fingers.

Now, the next player swings the invisible bat.
The sixth player (and depending on how many
are playing, that player may be going for the
second time already) must act out the sign made
by the Cricket referee when a player hits a six-
run hit. This is merely holding your arms in the
air like a touchdown in American football, only
your palms face outward.

Now, every fourth person does the four-hit
sign, but so will each player on a number with
four in it, like 14 or 49. The same goes for the
sixes. In cases like the number 24, which is a
multiple of six and four, the four in the number
wins out.

Players, believe it or not, must keep the count
in their heads. Vocalizing is strictly prohibited
and, like messing up the swing or the sweep,

will merit the bloody bastard a trip to his foaming glass of Carlton or Victoria Bitter. In the likely event of an error, the count begins at one.

Commentary:

You can thank the krazee kangaroos in Melbourne, Australia, for pulling this one from their pouches, although I gathered that they picked it up off some student backpackers from Great Britain. The grand thing about this game is, not just that you can play it for an hour and still be having a peak time, but you can be sure such a game would never originate in the States, where the only thing that would sell slower than a Cricket match would be a Milli Vanilli reunion tour . . . unless you could bring eggs and spoiled fruit.

The Insult Game

Requirements:

- ability to think on your feet
- ephemeral indifference to another's feelings

Directions:

One player begins by insulting another player. That player now either responds to the first player with an insult or chooses to insult another player.

Each insult must maintain the particular theme or image pattern set forth by the preceding insult. If it does not, or if the player can't mount a satisfactory insult immediately upon being insulted, that player must drink. The player who threw the insult that stumped the drinking player begins the game.

Players who cannot sufficiently respond must drink for their ineptitude. That floundering player then begins the game with any insult she cares to deliver. Remember, each insult must come on the heels of the one before it. Any substantial delay will be cause enough for stopping the game while the culprit enjoys a drink.

Commentary:

Best either to set guidelines for what's appropriate and what's not, or to agree that everything's fair game. In this way, deep-seated insults are not answered with angry fists, and everyone finishes the game wearing perky smiles.

I remember the night I learned the Insult Game. Cedric and Gina, a fellow hockey player and a coworker respectively, were involved in a brutal shouting match that spared nothing. An outside observer would have predicted a fight, and I know Cedric well enough to know he'd have fought her, no problem. However, a mutual admiration developed, and the two went home together that night. Sunset, the end.

Cardinal Puff

Requirements:

- 1 big communal cup

Directions:

Fill the cup to capacity and set it before the player who agrees to go first. Players are competing, essentially, against themselves, since only one person is playing at a time.

Cardinal Puff is like a long monologue you need to memorize for drama class, and in order to pass, you must know it to the letter. Since that's the case, it would be better for me to script it for you as though it were a Broadway play.

You: "Here's to the Cardinal's first puff of the evening." *Grip the cup using your forefinger and thumb only, gently tapping the cup to the table once before drinking. When finished with the one drink, set down the cup and tap the tabletop with your right forefinger once, then your left forefinger once. Tap underneath the table with your right forefinger once, and then the left once. Stomp your right foot to the floor and then the left. Rise from your seat and back down once.*

Player: "Here's to the Cardinal's second puff puff of the evening."
Mimic the ritual described above, except

everything must be done twice, that is, two fingers on the cup—excluding the thumb—two cup taps, two long sips, two finger taps per finger, two foot stomps, two seat risers.

Player: "Here's to the Cardinal's third and final puff puff puff of the evening."
Now times everything by three. The difference with this third time is that the player, using three sips, must now finish the beverage in the cup until that blasted cup is bone dry.

Player: "Once a Cardinal, always a cardinal."
Turn the cup upside down for a few seconds and then back. The judge checks the table for liquid. If there is none and the table is dry, congratulations. If there are stray droplets, sorry. Hang your head in humility, curse the heavens, and start from the top.

Commentary:

Drinking game aficionados will forever question my decision to print the rules to Cardinal Puff, since this game truly exemplifies the charm of the oral tradition. Admittedly, the best way to learn this game is by trial and error, but this is a how-to book and how-to books explain things. Enjoy.

Still, I suggest reading the rules on your own and then introducing it to your group, allowing them to learn the hard way. I learned the hardest way, by watching two others play it and then trying unsuccessfully many times to mimic them. It was a long, unsightly night for my sorry self. But, much like a bicycle, a hockey slapshot, or, for guys, the secret to longer intercourse, once you learn it you will never forget it.

The Vegetable Game

Requirements:

- nothing, not even your teeth (in fact, you're better off without them)

Directions:

Every player picks a vegetable, like arugala, or crisp celery, or carrot sticks. Make sure everyone knows everyone else's chosen vegetable. The object is, in the style of Thumper, to say the name of your vegetable and then say the name of another person's vegetable *without showing your teeth*. When that other person's vegetable is named, she must then name her vegetable and someone else's. A player loses a round if they cannot successfully name both vegetables without revealing their pearly whites. Laughing almost always determines the loser.

Commentary:

Okay, I know. Simple. Stupid. Inane. You're far too intelligent for this. You're in Mensa or something equally pretentious, right? Or you're a proud college grad, or you can play Iron Butterfly's "In-A-Gadda-Da-Vida" on the guitar left-handed and paint like Monet with your right. But all those flashy skills that make you class president or the date that a parent wants to meet won't help you here. This is equality under the pour spout.

5

FREEDOM IN THE GREAT OUTDOORS

GAMES TO BE PLAYED AWAY FROM THE TABLE

Ah, the great outdoors . . . a fantastic place to get shit-faced, where the cool green grass tickles the soles of your bare feet; the afternoon sun beats down on you brutally, giving you heat stroke and making you regret those turkey dogs; the chilly, refreshing beverages that seem to offer such respite from the sky's yellow flame taste great but are actually busy depleting you of hydration; a wave of fresh spring air whirls in your lungs, refuting in one breath all that cloudy talk of smog; and childhood memories of Little League, or in my sorry case T-ball, flood back in a warm flush, making you feel special again, giving you that much-needed sense that you've done something with your life, even if it was that lucky double you hit as a tot.

That's why games outdoors, while easily the smallest minority of drinking games, are often the best. It's easy to sit inside and forget about life, to live like a beached whale in your recliner and neglect the fresh air that beckons the kid in us all. But don't do it; don't let the bastards weigh you down! I, your drinking game guide, have a plan for you: sign up at a temp service. It's great, like being employed when you need cash and being unemployed when you've got a little saved up and don't give a damn. In your spare time you can practice that blossoming snapshot, or melodic minor scales on a rented oboe. Then when your friends get off work, those foolish workin' stiffs who have yet to figure it out, you can gather them up and play Drink the Can or Scavenger Drunk with newfound stamina for life.

And as your life winds down in the twilight years, instead of pay stubs and a pathetic couch potato retirement clogging up the blood vessels to your brain and making you comatose, you're learning Robert Johnson tunes on a beat-up Rickenbacker and musing over how, by chasing your heart's passions and not selling out, you managed to live a rich life.

In fact, "the great outdoors" is a good metaphor for loosening the collar and sniffing the flowers. And as you play drinking games outside, you begin to feel that life is not among cheap, pushover cubicles with their standard-issue desk accompaniment and the flourishing bacteria trapped in the hotbox of climate control. Instead, games outside are where mud slithering cold and wet between your toes evokes a careless giggle, and where not even the stark blue atmosphere above, dashed with an occasional, carefree white cloud drifting by, can stop a fly ball.

Bat Races

Requirements:

- X baseball bats (one per team)
- X number of cups (one per player)

Directions:

Find an open space to play, far from sharp objects or hidden sprinkler heads. Divide evenly into teams and designate a starting line. In front of each team and ten feet away, lay down the bat. Ten feet beyond that, line up all the cups on the grass, making sure all cups are full. Now, each team gathers behind the starting line in single-file order. On your mark . . . get set . . . ROCK!

The player runs to the bat, stands it up and puts his forehead to it. Now, he circles the bat ten times. When finished, he must run to the cups and finish one. Then he returns and slaps the hand of his next teammate in line. The winning team is the one that . . . well, forget it. There are no winners in Bat Races.

Commentary:

You can imagine how many modifiers one can add to Bat Races. I won't lie to you: in my own opinion, this is a heinous game. All that spinning over the bat seems harmless on the page, but actually doing it is pretty grisly.

During the prosperous 1980s you could've played Bat Races French Caribbean style, where it was included in an afternoon frolic under the sun called the "liquor picnic." There, when your teammate reached you, the two of you switched bathing suits before you could run your leg. This is part Reaganomic excess plus part *Animal House* theory plus those naked Françaises comin' at you live. If this is your thing, or if you want it to be, enjoy.

Sloshball

Requirements:

- a baseball diamond
- a keg

Directions:

Divide players into two teams. At each of the bases, including home plate, fill quite a few cups with the day's beverage of choice. Fill them only half full, if that much. Just like that, you're ready to play Sloshball, a bastardization and a damn mockery of America's favorite sport. Just keep in mind that you're a ball player now. You have certain responsibilities, such as whining about your paltry three million a year, stubbing your toe and relaxing on the DL, and most important of all, forgetting that it's the *fans* who pay your salary.

From here on out, play baseball. However, each time you round a base, you drink one of the cups. You can not advance until this is done.

Commentary:

Lots of variations are known around the country for this one, and that isn't surprising. Some people like to plant a keg at second base; others demand a full twelve ounces be finished at each base. Either way, I'm sure you'll find there's nothing quite like mixing America's favorite pastime with America's favorite pastime.

Note: Unless you live within walking distance of a diamond, designate a driver.

Drink the Can

Requirements:

- 1 large tumbler or comparable cup

Directions:

Fill the tumbler to capacity with guess what? And place it in a central position in the neighborhood. Now, if someone doesn't volunteer to be "it" for the first round, which no one will, either roll dice to determine "it," shoot a basketball, or do anything you can think of to figure out "it."

All those not "it" run and hide around the neighborhood while "it" counts to fifty. Does this sound familiar? Yes it does, but here comes the curveball you knew was coming: the object of those hiding is to make it to the tumbler and, like nimble Jack, leap over it. If they succeed, "it" must drink a portion of the tumbler. If "it" catches a player, *that* player must drink from the tumbler. The first player caught is automatically "it" for the next round. The remainder of the tumbler must be finished by the final player if he's caught by "it," *or* "it" must finish the tumbler if the last player makes the leap.

If "it" catches no one, "it" will be "it" again. That's an awful lot to be drinking, especially when you've got to have your wits about you!

Commentary:

A take on your favorite childhood game, Kick the Can, and for this reason alone you gotta love it. No matter how old you get, there's still a great feeling of accomplishment when, from your resourceful hiding place, you hear an exhausted "it" cry out that famous, nonsensical white flag of words, "Alli-alli-auction-free!"

A variation known among the Californians who conceived this is as follows: each person in hiding has a beverage that they must finish before getting caught; if they do not, they must finish it upon capture and then finish another of whatever they're drinking. Enjoy!

Since I am your guide and I care about you, here's a tip: these aren't the carefree suburban days of old. Don't hide in your neighbor's bushes if your neighbor is one of the new breed of American paranoids who keeps a loaded gun under his pillow and his porch is trip-wire booby-trapped. This game's cool, but not *that* cool.

Bowling for Beers

Requirements:

- a bowling alley

Directions:

This hellraiser is measured by frame and quantified by pin. So if you're rotten at bowling, which I am, you're gonna have a hell of a time.

Each player completes their frame. The person who has knocked down the most pins does not have to drink. Those players who have earned a

lower score than the frame's winner must drink
the amount of pins they've left standing.

A gutter ball, a pathetic and laughable gutter
ball worthy of group ridicule, earns the roller the
right to consume one-half of his beverage. If he
hits a second gutter ball, he finishes said beverage. The lesson here is, and let it apply to life in
general—avoid the gutter.

If you score a spare, you hand out as many
drinks to any one opponent as pins you knocked
down on your second ball to earn the spare.

Scoring a stately strike guarantees every other
player a drink, unless another player scores a
strike, in which case all players with strikes do
not drink, while those without do.

Commentary:

Stay far, far away from league night, which is
hellish no matter which American city you find
yourself in while you bowl for beers.

We used to play this contest at a twenty-four-
hour bowling alley . . . twenty-four hours! And
we were never the only bowlers during the
night's wee hours, which is even more amazing
than twenty-four-hour bowling.

Oh, and please designate a driver. If you're
the big loser in Bowling for Beers, you may find
upon leaving the bowling alley that you still
can't stay out of the gutter.

Relay Race of the Damned

Requirements:

- a full house (preferably six players per team)
- a busload of ten or twelve ounce cups with a wide base
- 2 large tumblers

Directions:

This is a three-part relay race meant for two teams, but if you've got more, that's fine.

Designate a starting line, then set up two small tables ten feet from the line. On each table, place two full cups of the afternoon's beverage per player. Then fill the tumbler and place it on the table as well.

Relay Race of the Damned then flows as follows:

Leg One: Teams line up single file at the starting line, each with a cup of beer (this is separate from what you've set on the tables). The relay starts when the players at the front of the line begin drinking. When they finish, they must balance the cup on their heads. Once firmly balanced, the second player follows suit, and then the third, and so on. When the last person is finished and all cups are balanced, your team can advance to the second leg.

Leg Two: The first player in line runs to the table, gets in a crablike, back-bending position, and balances two of the cups on her stomach. She then must walk in that position back to the line, where the next player drinks one of the cups while pouring the other one into the crab's mouth. When both drinks are done, that next player follows suit until all players have gone and all drinks are finished.

Leg Three: Your team must now form a human pyramid. While in the pyramid, a player on the bottom will begin drinking from the tumbler. By drinking and then passing it on all the way to the top, the player atop the pyramid will finish it off.

The first team to do so has won the Relay Race of the Damned, but not without a price. In other words, both winners and losers will probably be in the same unsteady hell.

Commentary:

This certainly reeks of Greek system wackiness, and while the first leg of this race is its own popular fraternity drinking game/activity called Boat Races, the rest is homegrown and home-tested; developed by yours truly and a few of the names listed at the beginning of the book.

The great thing about any relay race is that you can always add another leg or alter its intensity if you like. If you want to be traditional you can add the ol' potato sack. If you want some nausea, add a somersault or two. Wanna meet the devil? Add Bat Races to the mix. A good representative for all drinking games, Relay Race of the Damned is as malleable as your imagination.

Bar Golf

Requirements:

- money
- a designated driver
- fortitude

Directions:

Obtain a designated driver and a map to nine bars. It's preferable if you can walk, but that isn't always the case. So, once you have both, you're ready to begin Bar Golf, the longest and possibly the most regrettable nine holes you'll ever play.

At each bar, pick out one particular drink that each player will consume. You will have fifteen minutes to drink it before heading to the next bar. Let's say you pick a margarita. If in the allotted fifteen minutes you drink one margarita, you're par for that "hole." If you squeeze two down in fifteen minutes, that's a birdie, and you're now one under. If you're a nut and drink three, it's an eagle, and you're two under. The game continues through the ninth bar, after which you go home and throw up.

Commentary:

Bar Golf doesn't have a winner, unless you get together a pot or something comparable for the player with the best score. The truth is, if you manage to stay par throughout the game, I think that's commendable. If you're one or two or three under for the game, there's a good chance you'll be under for the rest of the night, and some of the next day too. You'll be playing the back nine in the can all morning, and that's hardly a fair reward for your efforts.

Scavenger Drunk

Requirements:

- money
- a designated driver

Directions:

In Scavenger Drunk you're not looking to bring home a green twist-tie, three Q-tips, a dog bone, and a slick rubber ribbed for her pleasure. In fact, instead of returning home with more that you left with, you should be coming home with a lot less; less discretion, less anger, less money, to name a few. That probably determines the winner, or better said, the one who lost the least (see loser).

Map out all the establishments that serve alcohol in your area. Naturally, it's preferred that they're all within walking distance so you won't need a designated driver, but this isn't always possible. Once you've mapped them out, create a scavenger hunt that will lead each team through the same bars and restaurants but at different times. At each bar, the players must finish the assigned drink before the bartender gives them the next clue (you'll be surprised at how cooperative bartenders will be). The clue should hint at the type of bar the players will patronize next. The winner will have arrived at the final bar and consumed her drinks before anyone else.

The final goal should be something like a cash pool gathered together by all the participants. So it might be best to establish an entry fee. As to what to do about who pays for the drinks at the bar, that's up to you. It can come out of the pool or the players can pay it themselves.

Commentary:

There may truly be no better drinking game than Scavenger Drunk. While slightly expensive, it's still a landmark. If possible, try and play it at your apartment complex, where you run from door to door looking for a beer or a shot of something in

particular. The first to return with labels or
crushed cans is the winner of the pool.

Just to reinforce it:

If you're driving from bar to bar, each team has a
designated driver. To compensate, the driver
should be able to play next time without an entry
fee, or something comparable.

6

HARD-CORE & HELLISH

GAMES GEARED TOWARD KICKING YOUR ASS

At some unknown time during the course of human history, it became a sign of tough-guy endurance for a man to outdrink his adversary. While this standard does not hold true for women, showcasing perhaps once and for all which is the wiser sex, there are nonetheless some equally brutish feminine exceptions. And so for years it was a good and attractive thing to drink much and belch more, setting the course for casualties of such an ill-fated bravado. The one-hundred-ten pounder who thought he could work over the starting fullback almost always ended up knees down on the bathroom floor, staring shamefully at his toilet water reflection like a sorry Narcissus, thankful that at the very least he didn't shit himself. Hardly an achievement to write home about.

Despite its overwhelming stupidity, male virility has been attached, albeit loosely, to drinking. This is a facet of the relationship between Darwinian survival and drinking games. In this case, the connection works backward. If we have a subject who *claims* to outdrink any and all, we might guess that his genes, while rugged to the alcohol bug, are potentially more bestial and less intelligent than most.

Any monster who ascends the kitchen table in grunts and proceeds to cash more beer in two minutes than you could finish in a night is no hero but a beer-bellied sloth of the future. So even though he may conquer us lightweights and become king of the jungle, he has not proven superiority in anything worthwhile. And while he's a late night mess, sloppy and bloated on the couch, swimming in the beer stains on his muscle shirt, we less ferocious losers are still going strong, content in our loss and feeling like maybe there are drinking game winners after all: the ones who know their limits and don't give two squirts about measuring their status on the unfounded basis of quantified drinking.

And so for this chapter I recommend the lightweights to take the next exit in our journey. Don't bother yourself here. Don't hide behind a pasteboard bravado, that same bravado that has gotten you in trouble before. We all need to acknowledge our limits. While it *is* certainly possible to limit the penalties on each of the following games, it does tend to compromise their integrity.

Consider this chapter the black diamond of the ski slopes, or Goofy at Disneyland holding out his paw, telling you you're just too short to cruise this ride. It is no great virtue to be a heavyweight; in fact, you spend more money. What fun is that, when in the end you piss it all away anyhow? Endure the jokes from those who think they're righteous in the universe because they polish off X number of Hamm's and a forty of the Kobra, and remember that in the end your liver is happier and you have extra cash to spend on things far more important than clear water brewed into amber water and bottled for your enjoyment.

But for all those convinced of your iron stomach and thick blood, indulge freely in the perils of this chapter, but don't be stupid about it. Falling Rock and Loose Gravel, for instance, coupled with One Hundred and One, can turn a night of solid good-time fun into a harrowing morning of the hair of the dog. Burnout and Beer Pong back-to-back will meddle with your innards and contort your once jolly smile into a portrait of anguish and grief. So, as you play along, try and remember the words of Falstaff, one of literature's great drinkers, when he said, "Discretion is the better part of valor."

Burnout

Requirements:

- X number of tall glasses
- X number of cigarettes
- X number of dimes
- X number of paper towels

Directions:

In preparation for Burnout, each player will fill their glass four-fifths full with—what else?— I'm not even gonna say it. Wet the rim of the glass with liquid. Place the paper towel over the top of the glass. Press down to make sure the liquid on the rim of the glass is soaking through. Tear away the paper towel, leaving only a piece of towel over the opening of the glass. Now gingerly place a dime in the middle. Light your smoke and take a drag, if you're into that kind of thing. Don't drag if you're not, because it's unhealthy and this book is doing backflips to make you a healthier, happier person.

Now, simultaneously, each player burns a hole in the paper towel. If it catches fire, and it might . . . blow it out! Then burn another hole. The first person to cause their dime to take a plunge must drink their beverage in its entirety. From here, YOU pick the exciting conclusion:

(a) All players start again. Reattach fresh paper towel and go for it!
(b) Continue until only one player's dime is left dry. That player, a clear-cut winner, doles out his ash-ridden beverage to the other sorry fops, and you begin again.

Commentary:

Nonsmokers need not apply. As expected, the room fills up with smoke, and it can get downright tough to function. If the weather's nice, I recommend sitting outside on the patio.

Burnout is meant to pummel you at the liver and the lungs. On account of this one-two punch, I am hesitant in getting too hyped about this game. I'm trying to look out for you, to be the most stalwart of guides. So acknowledge the surgeon general's warning against smoking and proceed with the cautious beer-drinking bravado that earned you that burgeoning beer belly in the first place.

Sink and Drink

Requirements:

- 1 pitcher
- 1 mug or cup that will float in liquid

Directions:

Fill up the pitcher to four-fifths capacity. Place the mug in the pitcher and balance it steadily.

Each player now pours a little of their individual beverage into the mug. They may choose to pour a little, say no more than a drop, or they may choose to pour a good amount. The object is to make the next person sink the cup. If that next person is you, refer to the title of this game . . . that's right! You sink? You drink! A full cup of the beverage, no less. Retrieve that sodden mug and scoop yourself a hearty helping. When finished, balance the mug once again and play until the pitcher is dry.

Commentary:

This game is Canadian; coming to you from college students in Montreal, home of the Habs and the new Molson Centre. Those krazee Canucks, who for years have given us nothing but NHL prospects and Rush albums, are coming at you with a zinger!

This contest has two American aliases: Sink the Battleship and Sink the Titanic, both of which require that you float a bottle cap and not a cup. But c'mon, that kind of wimpiness is what you opened this chapter to avoid, remember? So lace up your ice skates and get ready for a *real* hip check!

Falling Rock and Loose Gravel

Requirements:

- 1 quarter
- 10 stackable cups (you'll have to make a pyramid, so they need to be about to the same size)

Directions:

Stack the cups into a pyramid: five cups comprise the bottom level, four cups make up the middle level, and a single cup crowns the construct. Now, fill up each cup with the amounts that correspond to the cup number.

Figure 4

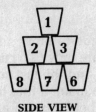

SIDE VIEW

TOP VIEW
NOTE: CUP #10 IS AT THE
CENTER OF THE BOTTOM LEVEL

The object is to shoot the quarter first into the top cup, hand it to an opponent to drink, and leave it off the pyramid. Then you shoot into the next four cups one by one, going clockwise from a designated point. If at any time you sink the quarter into a cup lower than the cup for which everyone is aiming, you must drink that cup and all the cups it supports, and then refill and replace them. As in standard Quarters, if a player fails to hit a cup, the quarter moves on. Also, three in a row constitutes a table rule.

When you arrive at the bottom five cups, you have two options. This book leans to the left, often giving you the consumer the right to choose, 'cause we're Americans and dammit if the Stars and Stripes doesn't give us that right!

Showcase Number 1: When the five bottom cups are left, employ the rules of Chandeliers (see Chapter 1). You may shoot for another's cup, and if you hit it, he must drink it, but the last to finish their cup if the communal cup (designated at this point as the cup in the center) is hit, must drink the communal cup.

Showcase Number 2: Continue to move in a clockwise fashion. When there are only two cups left—the communal middle cup and the last surrounding cup—the last player to make it into the surrounding cup gets to assign both cups to any player or players.

Commentary:

This is yet another homespun contest, altogether too hard-core for the Quarters chapter. The name derives rather loosely from your quarter tinkling down through all that glass and the sorry state of your innards the following morning. It could also be called Cheops Quarters or Twenty-Five-Cent Sphinx, or whatever you decided to call it. Names, rules . . . they just don't really matter.

Beer Pong

Requirements:

- Ping-Pong table with paddles, net, and a ball
- 4 cups

Directions:

Fill all cups half full and place one at each corner of the Ping-Pong table. Now, play Ping-Pong, scoring as you would a normal game.

However, there are some alterations. Plopping the ball into either of your opponents' cups forces the ploppee to chug the cup to depletion. The ploppee must then spit out the ball. You may also force your opponent to drink merely by hitting one of this cups with the ball. In addition, any time a regular point is scored, the loser must drink.

Commentary:

Who remembers Pong, the home-computer game forefather to everything from the Atari

2600 to the Nintendo 64? Glory. It's a wonder when you look back to rediscover the things that held your interest at one point in your life.

Fortunately, Beer Pong is more thrilling. It isn't merely the computer game brought into the third dimension. This game's got it all: sportiness for the health nut, paddles for you S&M freaks, a ball into a cup for basketball fans, a net for the fishermen or for computer nerds, an easy-to-store folding table for the practical, and challenge for those with great competitive spirit. And if that isn't enough to get you to lace up your table tennis shoes, then maybe you're just an insatiable party pooper and you should just go home.

Note: If you find yourself turning half the table upward and playing Beer Pong against yourself, seek help.

One Hundred and One

Requirements:

- 1 shot glass

Directions:

The directions are simple and the game sounds easygoing, but don't let it deceive you! Every minute on the minute, take a single shot of beer. Even though you may crave another sooner, wait until the minute has elapsed and then take it.

The point, if it deserves such a dignified term, is to make it to 101 one shots of beer in 101 minutes, without sending it back up. Ever.

Commentary:

So far, I know of no one who could make it. I'm sure you're out there, but I try not to play drinking games with your kind. I can admit without shame that you're way too hard-core for me. And since I can admit that, you should probably admit that if you can make it to 101, you have a problem and you need some serious help. In other words, the beer shits induced by this menacing beast should be the least of your worries.

A friend from UC Santa Barbara told me about the "The 72-Hour Club," also known as "The True 100 Club." In order to be a member of this classy, upper echelon, you must drink 100 beers in 72 hours. Great God, people, don't try this at home or anywhere ever in your life. Don't succumb to the peer pressure or the temptation of such undesirable fame. Guys, the chicks don't care if you can do it. And girls, the dudes would rather you couldn't. If ever you feel tempted, just do the math: that's one beer every forty-three minutes and twelve seconds. Inhuman. And totally absurd. From what deep, sordid cellar of the human soul did this club climb out?

7

MISCELLANEOUS MAYHEM

GAMES WHOSE RULES FIT NO PARTICULAR CHAPTER

An old antique shop, a single-family garage sale, Martha's bric-a-brac: these seeming scrap heaps filled with dusty nostalgia often yield up treasures of great worth whose time has already come and gone. But while some see no use in such lonesome jewels, others, upon uncovering them for a steal, consider themselves luckier than the person who found Tutankhamen or the Joe who bought that three-dollar Picasso.

You used to be able to hit a residential garage sale on some sunny Sunday and walk away having paid five dollars for a gramophone similar to the bamboo one the Professor built, or the one Mike Brady rebuilt. The scrap heaps of the country still produce hidden wonders. Imagine entering a used record shop and finding a stack of priceless imports at forty-nine cents apiece, or a bookshop with a pristine copy of the Alexander Pope translation of *The Iliad*. Could you really contain your blood pressure upon such discoveries?

I'm getting to know you pretty well, you excitable demon, and I don't think you could.

For that thrilling reason, I urge you not to dismiss this miscellaneous chapter with the same haughty shrug you give the general store or the thrift shop. Within these grooves are some real rockers and a hearty dynamo or two, more than capable of giving Krazee You and Your Animals heart palpitations and making you wag your long, Gene Simmons–inspired tongues in devilish bliss.

Most of the contests in this chapter are drinking game staples. TV Junkies is vastly well-known, and is generally found at smaller gatherings, along with Board Games. Caps, on the other hand, is a popular fraternity game and "big party" favorite. DC Bob is a newcomer to the field of drinking games, but destined someday to join its chapter counterparts in the hall of fame, on whatever day that questionable temple to indulgence is erected.

TV Junkies

Requirements:

- the omnipresent television

Directions:

Find a show you either truly like or love to hate, like *Melrose Place*, *90210*, or *Knight Rider*. Now sit back and do what we Americans do best: rot in front of the television. (Note: It may feel good to sit in the recliner and play this game, but please resist—it's the kiss of death!)

Each player chooses one character and drinks every time that character appears on screen. You also drink if, in the same scene, your character shows up in a different camera angle.

Commentary:

If you're going to use a prime-time soap like *Melrose*, I don't recommend drinking every time the writers have scripted a line so shockingly pitiful that you bust out laughing; you'll be bloated before either the first commercial break or before the plot collapses, whichever comes first.

However, it is important to designate some opportunities for social drinking. For example, let's say you settle down for *Different Strokes* reruns. Every time Arnold Jackson spits the perennial studio audience favorite, "Whatchou talkin' 'bout, Willis?" you should probably drink. Each time Mr. Drummond spews some bogus, exhausted sitcom moral, drink. The Gooch wants to kick Arnold's ass? By all means, drink to that!

Note: Hi Bob is probably the most well-known drinking game TV show (from *The Bob Newhart Show*). The gag is that every time someone says "Hi Bob!" you drink. This occurs more often than you could imagine, but never seems to get old. I recommend Hi Bob if, for no other reason, it's a hell of a show!

DC Bob

Requirements:

- 1 very large tub (5 gallon recommended)
- 8 tennis balls
- 1 non-water-soluble pen

Directions:

Fill your tub to capacity with water. On four of the tennis balls write the letter D. On the other four write C. Now, for each set of four, write the following values, one per ball: 1/4, 1/2, 3/4, F. Put them in the tub. Toss in some ice cubes for an extra laugh or two, and you're ready to begin.

Player One approaches the tub and bobs for a tennis ball. He rears his head out of the water with the ball labeled D 3/4. So, that sorry fool must drink (thus the D) three-quarters of his beverage and be happy about it. Player Two approaches. She pulls out the ball labeled C 1/2. She now chooses (thus the C) another player to consume one-half his or her beverage. If in the allotted ten seconds a player is not able to retrieve a ball, the penalty is a standard drink.

Commentary:

Here we go again. The bastardization of yet another childhood favorite. It would appear as though in the kingdom of drinking games, nothing is sacred. Somewhere along the line, everything from our national pastime to the sunny days and friendly nights of youth and innocence will be desecrated. And for what? Some hearty snickering, a little ridicule perhaps, a buzz followed by the hair of the dog the next morning. Once more, history and memory are perverted . . . enjoy!

Ladle

Requirements:

- 1 good-sized ladle
- 1 bottle cap
- X spoons
- 1 small saucepan
- any timepiece armed with a timer and alarm

Directions:

Fill the saucepan with your favorite beverage, making sure it remains deep enough to scoop with the ladle. Hand out a spoon to each player. You're ready to begin.

Set the timer for one minute. Players must pass the bottle cap from spoon to spoon, making sure at each pass that the bottle cap is turned over. In other words, when Player A has the cap in her spoon label up, it must be flipped over in passage to Player B to reveal the underside. This occurs in rapid succession until the timer goes off.

When that timer does go off, the player in possession of the cap must put his spoon down and take the ladle firmly in his hand. (During each passing, it's the player who's passing that will be responsible when the timer goes off.) The player to the ladle holder's left will position a spoon close to the bottom of the saucepan, handle out, and place the cap somewhere along the handle. She will then attempt to flip the cap off the spoon and into the saucepan. The player holding the ladle is attempting to intercept the cap before it reaches the saucepan. Behold a list of the consequences to various outcomes:

1. *Player catches cap in ladle label down*: Player removes cap, takes a scoop from the saucepan, and drinks it from the ladle. Game resumes.

2. *Player catches cap in ladle label up*: (This is more uncommon.) Player removes cap and gives ladle to player of her choice to take one scoop from the saucepan. Game resumes.

3. *Player misses cap and it splashes in saucepan label down*: Player with ladle, like a box of Raisin Bran, has two scoops. Game resumes.

4. *Player misses cap and it splashes in saucepan label up*: Player with ladle enjoys one scoop and may give away the other scoop. Game, of course, resumes.

5. *Player misses cap and cap misses saucepan:* Unacceptable. Keep shooting until 1 through 4 occurs.

Commentary:

Legend has it, if we are to trust the tongue of Melissa, my source for this game, that Ladle was passed along by a mysterious party crasher everyone courteously accepted as a friend of someone else's. And when this clever interloper left, it was discovered that no one knew who in the hell he was. A handsome stranger (he was beautiful, according to Melissa) now walks the night with the root stocks of this game tucked neatly away in his head.

I'm serious about this, by the way. Generally, finding the source for most games is impossible, especially the classics, since they've been around for so long. In addition, drinking games follow an oral tradition, making it extremely difficult to nail down any sure thing. In this case, though, the enigmatic drinker acted almost as though he was making it up as he went along. Who is this Zorro figure with the sharp gray matter? And what other gems does he keep locked up in his kitchen-table mind, only to release to unassuming strangers around an unfamiliar table?

Tupperware Two-Step

Requirements:

- 1 Tupperware lid
- players must wear pants with loose pockets

Directions:

Stand in a circle, hip-to-hip, in whatever order you feel most comfortable. Go on, get cozy. Don't be shy.

Now, each player will take his or her hands and place them in the pockets of the people standing on either side (guys, show some discipline—you're not sixteen anymore). Now, players pass the Tupperware lid from hand to hand without taking their hands from their pockets. Do it quickly. If it's dropped, both players involved in the boner remove their hands and drink.

Commentary:

Sex 'n' drugs 'n' rock 'n' roll. Ian Dury's standard brought to life under the auspices of a college drinking game. In fact, make a few Caribbean-influenced changes to Bat Races, add a little Tupperware Two-Step, and you've got yourself a scene right out of Led Zeppelin's *Houses of the Holy* tour, or a statement to the establishment made by peace-totin' free lovers at one of those heralded early seventies kink parties.

However, I will take no responsibility for any subsequent postparty stupidity, and will not hold your hand as you make the historic "walk of shame" home under that awfully bright and revealing morning sun.

Board Games

Requirements:

- any board game

Directions:

Simply put, make a successful marriage between the spirit of the rules of different games in this book and the rules of your board game. You may even want to refer to the parameters set forth in the introduction to help you out.

Commentary:

As you're sifting through your closet, try to remember that games like Risk prove pretty rotten for this kind of thing. The more active the game, meaning the more involved you are, the more physical it gets, and the less complex thinking required, the better. The Hungry Hippo, for example, works magically. Mouse Trap will make you piss your pants. Twister is, needless to say, an ass-kicker, provided you're playing with the right people and the beer goggles are on tight. Life may prove too heavy, since it may be what you're trying to escape by playing drinking games. Monopoly is a disaster. Keep it on the shelf.

Best advice: Apply the discretion you've developed though the course of this book in picking a board game, and it will not fail you.

Caps

Requirements:

- X cups
- 10 bottle caps (for every two players)

Directions:

Generally, only two players participate in Caps, but go ahead and break the rules; you only live once, and lord knows you're wacky enough!

Split up your caps equally. Sit on the floor a fair distance from each other and place the cup between your legs. In fact, nuzzle your new friend right up against your groin. Go on, it feels great. Do this simple gesture and Caps becomes the game that keeps on giving.

Now, position a bottle cap between your thumbs. In other words, put your fingertips together so all corresponding fingers are touching. The object is to fling the cap into your opponent's cup. Do this, and she drinks. Miss, as you no doubt will, take a drink, and now it's her turn. If she can get three of her five bottle caps into your cup in one round, you have to consume a full beverage. None of this "take a sip" crap; the whole thing goes. Then gather up the caps and play again.

Commentary:

At Hastings College in Nebraska, according to alumna Nancy Farmer, Caps is almost as popular as detasseling the cornfields. And who knows, maybe there's a great drinking game in that activity somewhere. Heed that call, Heartlanders!

Caps tournaments exist, believe it or not. The way they often work is that people will operate in teams, sitting on the carpet with their legs stretched out in a V. Their feet will meet the feet of another player sitting the same way, and the competition will be to see how many caps your team can sink in a designated amount of time. Imagine the tremendous sense of accomplishment you'll feel at the end of the night when you recall that you alone sunk twenty-two caps, aiding your team to a fabulous overtime victory. That would be so special; a goose-bump frenzy, followed by the adoration of your peers and very possibly some groupie-inspired action later in the night.

And admit it, guys and girls: often, you're playing drinking games because somewhere down the line you're looking to see some action. I can admit that I wrote this book because I wanna be a rock star, so you too can admit to your misguided dreams and goals.

So here they were, fifty games in all, part powerhouse, part mellow, all rock. The mood is always so somber when saying good-bye, but I know we drinking game aficionados live in each other's hearts long after the last quarter is shot or the final cap is flung. So keep plugging away. Keep looking for that special twist that can turn your ho-hum family game into a national party pastime.

And keep looking for me on the cover of *Rolling Stone* with the rest of the band, posing like indulgent, decadent rock stars with our fingers up like the devil's horns, inciting sex and other social destruction like all *good* rock stars should!